Maggie is a black cat.

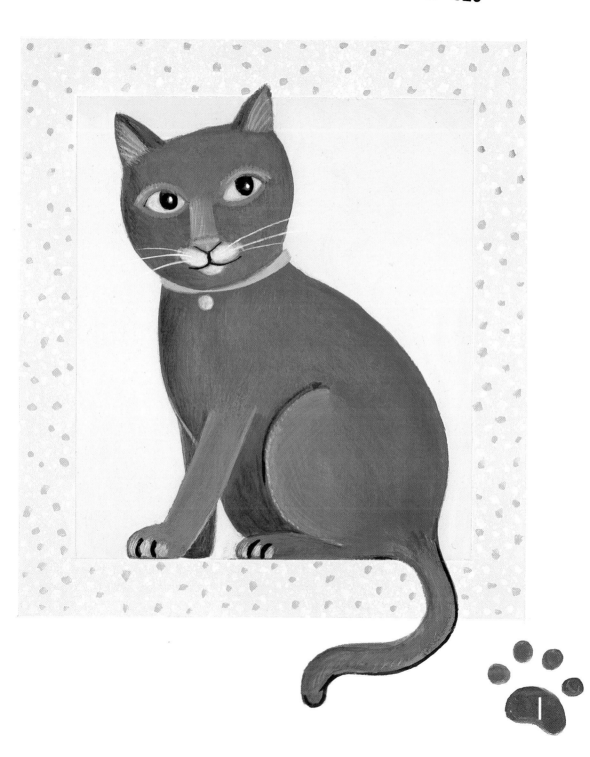

1

Danny is her pal.

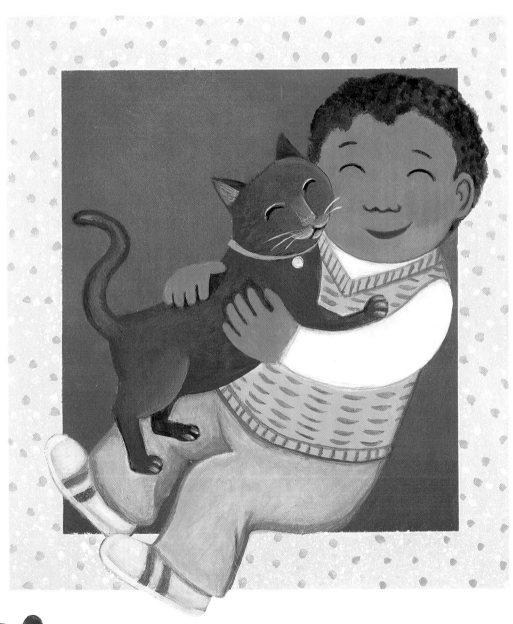

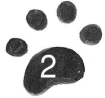
2

Maggie can act like a dog.

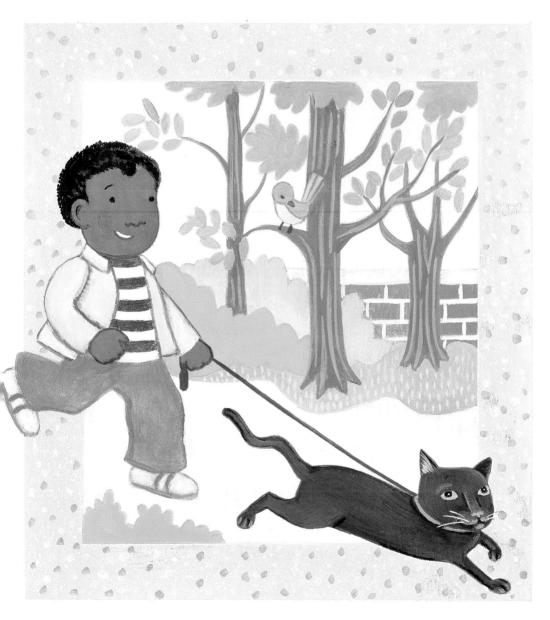

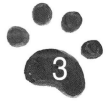
3

Maggie can wag her tail for Danny.

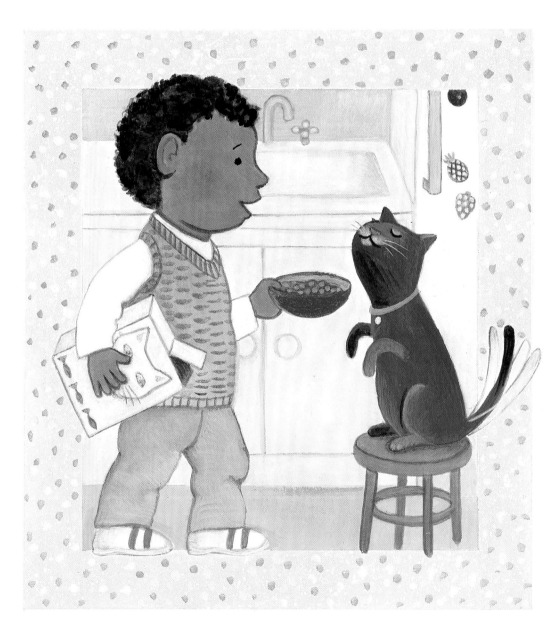

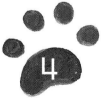
4

Maggie can catch a ball from Danny.

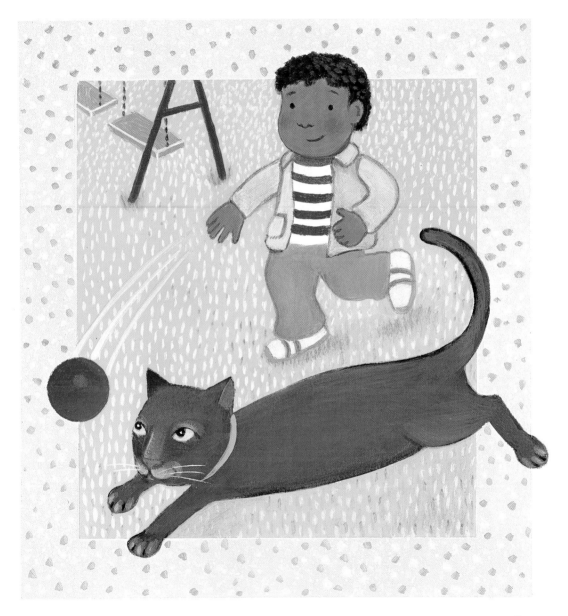

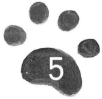

Maggie can dance for Danny.

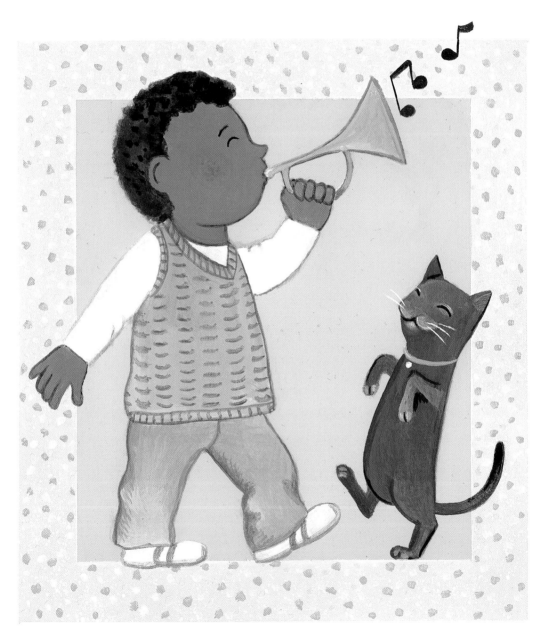

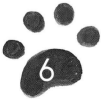

But when Danny goes to school, . . .

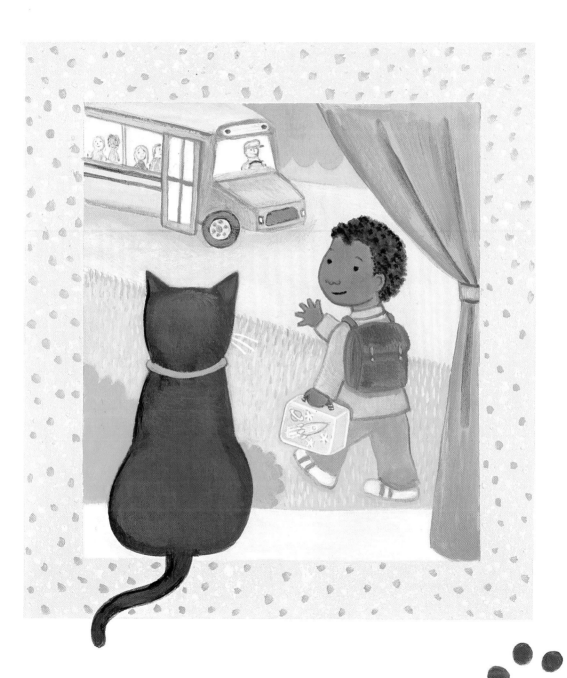

Maggie acts like a cat!

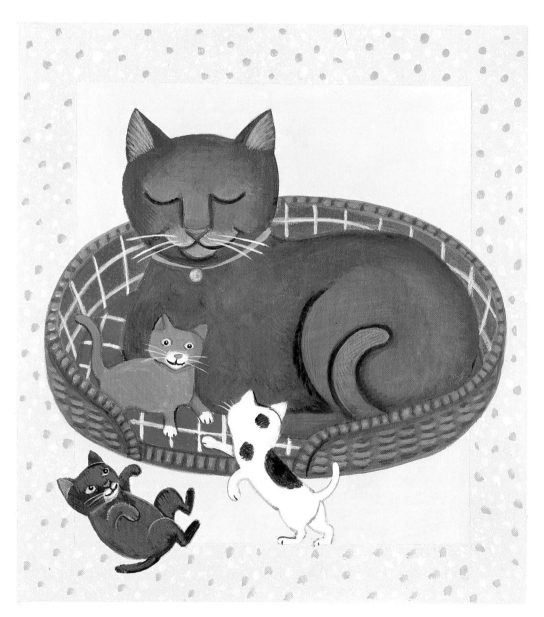

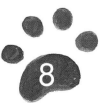